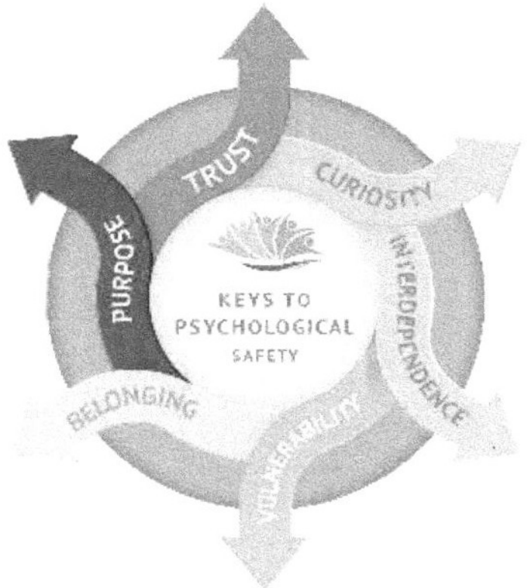

Psychological Safety Decoded: The Essential Primer for Leaders & HR Champions

by
David C Winegar

Table Of Contents

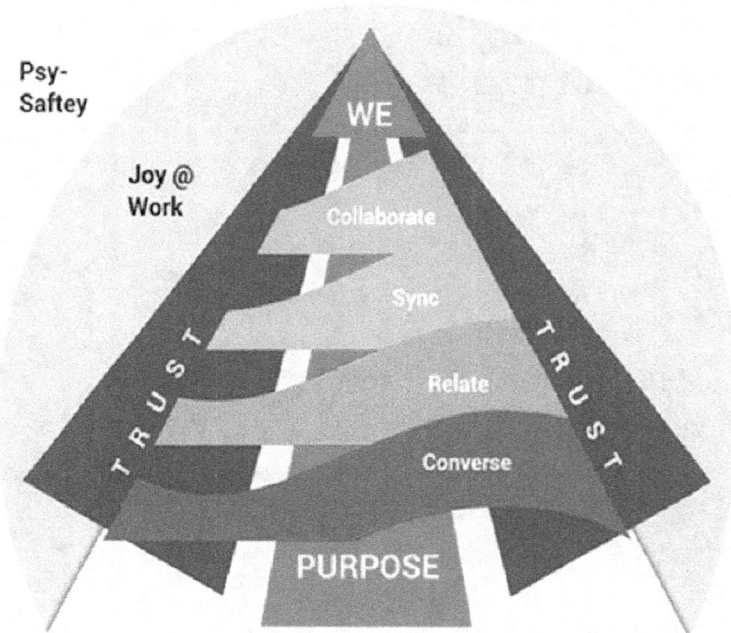

Chapter 1: Introduction

Introduction: The New Frontier of Modern Workplaces

In a world increasingly shaped by rapid technological advancements, evolving societal norms, and the unpredictability of global events, the one constant that seems to govern our collective experience is change. Our professional environment, a microcosm of the larger world, is no exception. As we stand at the intersection of tradition and innovation, one term has come to the forefront, promising a transformative approach to how we perceive and navigate our workplaces: psychological safety.

But before we delve into this pivotal concept, it's essential to understand the context. Today's workplaces are vastly different from those of our predecessors. We've transitioned from industrial-centric economies to knowledge-based ecosystems. The hierarchies of old are being replaced, if not complemented, by more flexible and inclusive structures. The "job for life" model has given way to dynamic roles, remote work, gig economies, and multifaceted career trajectories. Yet, amidst this dizzying pace of change, one thing remains clear: the human element, with all its complexities, hopes, fears, and aspirations, remains at the core of any organizational endeavor.

So, as the boundaries of what we know as 'work' expand and blur, the questions we must ask are: How do we ensure that our workplaces are not just efficient, but also humane? How do we cultivate environments where people, the most valuable assets of any organization, feel empowered, valued, and above all, safe?

Enter psychological safety, a term that, while not new, has become increasingly relevant in recent years. It's the bridge between efficiency and empathy, productivity and well-being, growth and integrity. However, to truly appreciate its significance, we need to journey back to the roots of organizational thinking.

Historical Roots

The early 20th century witnessed the rise of Taylorism or Scientific Management, where workplaces were driven by efficiency, and workers were often viewed as mere cogs in the vast industrial machine. While this approach led to significant advancements in productivity and scale, it also created environments that were often impersonal and dehumanizing. Employees were valued for their outputs, not for their individuality.

Fast forward to the latter half of the century, and we began to see a shift. Influenced by psychological and behavioral sciences, there was a growing realization that employee well-being directly impacted organizational success. Maslow's hierarchy of needs and Herzberg's two-factor theory, among others, emphasized the role of psychological factors in motivation and job satisfaction.

Yet, the journey was just beginning. The close of the 20th century and the dawn of the 21st brought with them challenges and opportunities that few could have predicted. The rise of the digital age, globalization, and the increasing emphasis on diversity and inclusion meant that workplaces were becoming more complex and interconnected than ever before.

The Modern Workplace: A Melting Pot

Today's professional ecosystem is a melting pot of cultures, generations, and ideologies. Baby boomers, Gen Xers, millennials, and Gen Zers all coexist in the same space, each bringing their unique perspectives and expectations. This diversity, while a strength, also presents challenges. How do you create an environment that caters to such a vast spectrum of needs and aspirations?

Moreover, the nature of work itself has transformed. With the increasing emphasis on services, information, and creativity, our jobs are less about following set procedures and more about innovation, problem-solving, and collaboration. Such roles require environments where risks are taken, boundaries are pushed, and occasionally, mistakes are made.

However, for employees to take these leaps, they need more than just technical tools or skills. They need an environment where they feel secure enough to venture into the unknown, confident that their efforts will be acknowledged, their achievements celebrated, and their mistakes viewed as learning opportunities.

Psychological Safety: The Keystone

This is where psychological safety emerges as the keystone of modern organizational structures. It's a term that captures the essence of what employees need to thrive in today's intricate professional maze.

But what is psychological safety? At its core, it's the belief that one can be oneself, without the fear of retribution or ridicule. It's about ensuring that every voice, regardless of its source, is heard and valued. It's about creating environments where feedback is constructive, not destructive; where diversity is celebrated, not just tolerated; where well-being is integral, not just incidental.

While this might sound idealistic to some, there's a growing body of evidence that underscores its tangible benefits. From enhanced innovation and productivity to reduced turnover and absenteeism, the positive outcomes of psychological safety are manifold.

Yet, as with all concepts, understanding its theory is just the beginning. The real challenge lies in its application. How do organizations, from fledgling startups to multinational behemoths, cultivate this elusive yet essential quality? How do leaders, often products of traditional hierarchical structures themselves, foster an environment of psychological safety? And most importantly, how do employees, each with their unique personalities, experiences, and aspirations, navigate and contribute to this paradigm?

The Journey Ahead

As we delve deeper into this subject, these are some of the questions we'll explore. Drawing from research, real-world case studies, and expert insights, we'll unravel the tapestry of psychological safety, examining its threads, understanding its patterns, and seeking ways to integrate it into our professional tapestry.

In essence, while the tools, technologies, and even the very nature of our jobs might change, our innate human need for understanding, connection, and safety remains unchanged. In the vast, intricate dance of organizational dynamics, psychological safety is the rhythm that can synchronize diverse steps into a harmonious ballet. It's not just a concept; it's a compass, guiding us towards workplaces where efficiency meets empathy, where growth is not just about scales and numbers, but also about people and their stories.

Join us on this journey, as we explore the realms of psychological safety, understanding its nuances, and seeking ways to make it a lived reality for all.

What is Psychological Safety?

In today's fast-paced, interconnected, and dynamically changing work environment, there's a term that stands tall in the corridors of organizational thought: "psychological safety." It represents a shift in our understanding of what truly drives success in the modern workplace. But before we immerse ourselves in its intricate depths, let's first lay the foundation of understanding.

The Definition

At its simplest, psychological safety describes an environment where individuals feel free to express their thoughts, opinions, and concerns without fear of retribution or ridicule. It's an environment of trust, mutual respect, and empowerment. But as with many things, simplicity is only the tip of the iceberg.

The Evolution and Its Roots

Tracing the genesis of the term takes us back several decades, as scholars of organizational behavior began recognizing the importance of individual perception in the workplace. However, the term skyrocketed in corporate consciousness mainly due to two factors.

Firstly, the iconic study spearheaded by Google, known as 'Project Aristotle.' In their quest to understand what makes certain teams more successful than others, the company's researchers found that the answer wasn't necessarily tied to the team's collective IQ, skill sets, or even the nature of individual roles. It was more about the environment the team functioned within. Teams that exhibited higher degrees of psychological safety outperformed their peers, proving that the team's interactions and mutual respect played pivotal roles in success.

Secondly, the nature of modern work itself. As tasks become more collaborative and less linear, it's not just about getting from point A to point B. The journey matters. This journey is paved with creativity, innovative ideas, and untested waters. And to navigate it, individuals need an environment that doesn't penalize them for stepping off the well-trodden path. Psychological safety ensures that an employee can venture into the unknown, experiment, and even fail, all in the pursuit of excellence.

Going Beyond the Surface

But psychological safety isn't just about the absence of fear. It's about the presence of positive behaviors and attitudes that create a fertile ground for growth. It's about:

- **Openness**: An environment where dialogue is not just encouraged but celebrated, where diverse opinions form a beautiful mosaic of collective wisdom.

- **Respect**: Where every voice, regardless of rank or experience, is valued.

- **Empathy**: Understanding that behind every team member is a person with dreams, fears, challenges, and strengths.

- **Trust**: The belief that the team will support, not sabotage; that they'll provide a safety net during leaps of faith.

Moreover, it's not about preventing conflict but about ensuring that conflicts are constructive, springing from a place of mutual respect and shared goals. It encourages disagreements, but in the pursuit of truth and betterment, not one-upmanship.

The Nuanced Difference

It's pivotal to understand that psychological safety is not synonymous with always being "nice" or maintaining perpetual harmony. It doesn't demand passive agreement but encourages active participation. It differentiates between avoiding constructive critiques (which can be detrimental) and avoiding harsh judgment or ridicule.

Let's consider feedback, for example. In a psychologically safe environment, feedback is frequent, forward-focused, and developmental. It's not about highlighting failures but about paving a path for future success. It's shared with care and received with an open mind. Contrast this with a toxic environment, where feedback feels like an attack, meant to belittle rather than build.

The Broader Organizational Impact

Psychological safety is not just an individual need; it's an organizational imperative. Organizations that champion this principle witness:

- **Higher levels of innovation**: Employees aren't shackled by fear, allowing them to think outside the box.
- **Improved retention rates**: People are more likely to stay where they feel valued and safe.
- **Enhanced collaboration**: Trust promotes cross-functional cooperation, breaking down silos.
- **Greater adaptability**: Safe environments promote a growth mindset, vital for navigating the turbulent waters of change.
- **Robust problem-solving**: Multiple perspectives come to the fore without the fear of judgment, leading to comprehensive solutions.

Challenges in Implementation

Understanding psychological safety and effectively embedding it into organizational culture are two different challenges. Implementation requires consistent effort. It necessitates leaders to not only "talk the talk" but to "walk the walk," setting examples through their actions. It means rooting out behaviors that stifle psychological safety and nurturing those that bolster it.

Towards a Brighter, Safer Tomorrow

As we stand at the crossroads of traditional hierarchical structures and a more inclusive, collaborative future, psychological safety lights the way. It calls for a reimagining of workplaces, where hierarchies don't dictate the value of opinions, where mistakes are stepping stones to mastery, and where every individual, irrespective of their role, feels seen, heard, and valued.

In essence, psychological safety is the lifeblood of future-forward organizations. It's more than a concept; it's a culture, a way of life, a commitment to the holistic well-being and success of every individual in the organization. In embracing it, we pave the way for not just successful organizations but thriving, vibrant communities of professionals.

The Evolution of Workplace Culture

From Assembly Lines to Open Spaces: A Historical Overview

The history of the modern workplace is both fascinating and intricate. Beginning in the late 19th and early 20th centuries, the Industrial Revolution marked a defining moment. Factories and assembly lines became the hallmark of progress. Employees were viewed less as individuals and more as parts of a massive, efficient machine. The primary workplace culture was built around productivity, efficiency, and hierarchies.

During this era, the workplace was characterized by strict schedules, limited worker rights, and clear divides between the management and the workers. It was an age of rapid urbanization and mechanization, where industrial moguls and factory owners held significant power, and the focus was largely on output and profit.

The Mid-20th Century: Emergence of Employee Rights and Corporate Responsibility

As society progressed into the mid-20th century, significant events like the World Wars and the Great Depression had profound impacts on workplace dynamics. Workers began to organize, demanding better working conditions, fair pay, and more humane treatment. This period witnessed the rise of trade unions, collective bargaining, and an increased focus on worker's rights.

Simultaneously, organizational theories and psychological insights began to suggest that a happy worker was a productive worker. Concepts such as Maslow's hierarchy of needs pointed towards the importance of fulfilling not just the physiological and safety needs, but also the psychological needs of esteem and belonging.

Workplace culture began to shift towards more inclusive environments. Company picnics, benefits, and team-building activities became more commonplace. The emphasis started moving from mere productivity to employee well-being and motivation.

Late 20th Century: Technology, Globalization, and the Birth of Modern Corporate Culture

The advent of computer technology and the internet in the late 20th century revolutionized workplaces. Physical boundaries started diminishing as organizations began to operate on a global scale. This period marked the birth of the 'modern corporate culture'. Open offices, flexible timings, and the initial inklings of remote work started to emerge.

A significant cultural shift was the increasing value placed on innovation and creativity over mere task completion. Companies like Google, Apple, and Microsoft, which prized innovation and valued their employees' unique contributions, became the gold standard. Work culture began emphasizing collaboration, continuous learning, and adaptability.

Diversity and inclusion also became focal points. Companies realized that diverse teams, bringing varied perspectives and experiences, were more innovative and effective. Workplace culture started evolving to be more accepting and inclusive, aiming to cater to employees from varied backgrounds, genders, and orientations.

The 21st century brought with it a digital revolution. Workplaces became increasingly virtual, leading to the rise of freelancers, digital nomads, and a globally interconnected workforce. The COVID-19 pandemic further accelerated the acceptance of remote work, making it a norm rather than an exception.

Another significant shift was the importance of purpose and values in the workplace. Employees, particularly the younger generation, began seeking more than just a paycheck. They sought purpose, a sense of contribution towards something larger than themselves. This led to a surge in mission-driven companies and a focus on corporate social responsibility.

Mental health and well-being became central. With increasing awareness about mental health issues, organizations began implementing policies and practices to support their employees' holistic well-being. Concepts like work-life balance and psychological safety came to the forefront.

The Future: Sustainable, Holistic, and Human-Centric Work Cultures

As we gaze into the future, the evolution of workplace culture points towards more sustainable, holistic, and human-centric environments. The lessons learned from history, combined with the challenges and opportunities of the present, are likely to shape a future where:

- **Sustainability** becomes a core tenet, with organizations focusing not just on profits, but also on their environmental and social impact.

- **Holistic well-being** encompasses not just physical health, but mental, emotional, and social well-being. Workplaces will likely focus on creating environments that nourish all aspects of their employees' lives.

- **Human-centric designs** will prioritize the human experience over mere efficiency. This could manifest in more flexible schedules, humane tech policies, and environments that foster creativity, collaboration, and connection.

In essence, the evolution of workplace culture is a testament to our collective journey. As society, technology, and our understanding of humanity evolves, so do our workplaces. They stand as reflections of our values, aspirations, challenges, and hopes for the future.

Chapter 2: The Science Behind Psychological Safety

Introduction to the Science of Psychological Safety

The quest for understanding psychological safety isn't just about gauging its impact on team dynamics or organizational success. Delving into its science helps elucidate the deep-rooted neurological and psychological processes that underpin human behavior in workplace settings. As we embark on this journey through the mind and its intricate functions, the compelling evidence of the importance of psychological safety becomes evident.

Page 37

In recent decades, the confluence of neuroscience and organizational psychology has illuminated many facets of human behavior in professional settings. No longer do we rely on anecdotal accounts; now, empirical research provides a robust framework for understanding. Thus, before we deep dive into the mechanisms and evidence, it's essential to understand the broader scientific landscape from which these insights emerge.

The subsequent sections will offer a window into the neurological processes that govern our reactions to safe and threatening environments, followed by an exploration of the tangible impacts these processes have on productivity and well-being.

The Neurological Perspective

Brain's Functioning: Threat, Reward, and Social Connections

At its core, our brain is a marvel engineered for survival. The limbic system, with the amygdala at its heart, plays a pivotal role in recognizing threats. When confronted with danger, a cascade of neurological events ensues, releasing cortisol and other stress hormones, triggering the 'fight or flight' response. However, in modern times, these threats are less about physical danger and more about perceived social or emotional threats.

Interestingly, our brains also have evolved reward pathways, primarily centered around the release of dopamine. These pathways light up during positive social interactions, moments of learning, or when feeling valued. Psychological safety, in essence, minimizes threats and enhances these reward responses.

Furthermore, research has illuminated that our brain treats social pain, akin to physical pain. An environment rife with criticism or exclusion can activate pain pathways, leading to tangible stress and anxiety. In contrast, environments characterized by positive social interactions bolster our brain's reward systems, leading to feelings of pleasure, motivation, and connection.

Impact on Productivity and Well-being

The Symbiotic Relationship Between Safety and Performance

Workplaces that nurture psychological safety aren't just beneficial for employees; they're a boon for organizational success. Several studies have demonstrated a robust correlation between teams that foster psychological safety and those that outperform their peers. Such teams aren't merely more productive; they're more innovative, adaptive, and engaged.

A central theme in this synergy is trust. An environment that breeds psychological safety is inherently one of trust. When employees trust their peers and superiors, they're more inclined to take risks, voice their opinions, and share novel ideas. This trust isn't one-sided. Leaders who trust their teams delegate effectively, fostering autonomy and ownership, leading to higher job satisfaction and enhanced performance.

Moreover, the implications of psychological safety extend beyond mere performance metrics. In such nurturing environments, employees report better mental health, reduced burnout, and overall enhanced well-being. Reduced stress levels, lower absenteeism, and higher job satisfaction are but a few benefits organizations reap when they prioritize psychological safety.

The Resilience and Agility Fostered by Safety

Modern organizations operate in a volatile, uncertain, complex, and ambiguous (VUCA) world. In such a landscape, resilience and agility aren't just desirable traits; they're imperative. Organizations that have embedded psychological safety into their ethos find themselves better equipped to navigate these challenges.

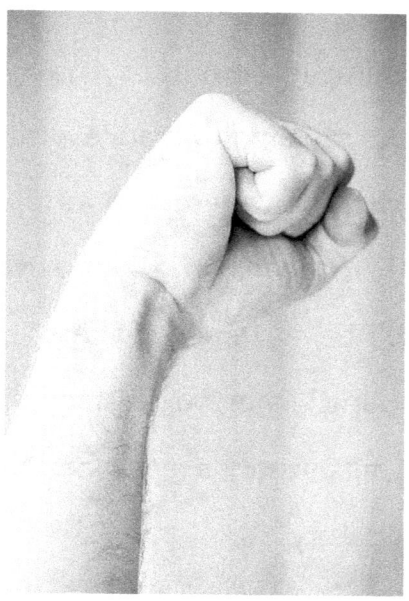

Resilience, often described as the ability to bounce back from adversity, is significantly enhanced in psychologically safe environments. Employees, unburdened by the constant stress of self-preservation, are free to channel their energies towards problem-solving, innovation, and collaboration. They become stakeholders in organizational success, leading to a collective resilience that can weather market downturns, internal challenges, or external crises.

Agility, the ability to rapidly adapt to changing circumstances, is another byproduct of psychological safety. In environments where open communication, feedback, and continuous learning are the norms, organizations can pivot effectively. By fostering a culture where failures are viewed as learning opportunities, organizations can iterate and evolve rapidly, staying ahead in the competitive landscape.

In this chapter, through the lens of science, the importance of psychological safety becomes unequivocally clear. As we move forward, armed with this knowledge, the path to fostering such environments becomes both a moral imperative and a strategic necessity.

Chapter 3: The Pillars of Psychological Safety

Trust and Mutual Respect

Trust is the foundation upon which all successful relationships are built, and the workplace is no exception. Within organizations, trust operates on multiple levels: employees need to trust their peers for collaboration, their superiors for guidance, and their subordinates for execution. This trust is a direct consequence of consistent behavior, transparency in decision-making, and the understanding that everyone is working towards a common goal.

However, trust doesn't flourish in isolation; it's deeply intertwined with mutual respect. It's about recognizing the intrinsic value in every individual, irrespective of their role, experience, or background. Mutual respect implies valuing diverse opinions, acknowledging the expertise of others, and treating everyone with dignity. In environments where respect is the norm, employees feel seen, valued, and, most importantly, safe.

The synergistic relationship between trust and mutual respect is dynamic. Like a muscle, it needs regular exercise. It's enhanced with every positive interaction, every kept promise, and every shared success. Yet, it's also fragile, susceptible to breaches, both intentional and inadvertent. Organizations that understand this dynamic nature invest continuously in nurturing it, reaping rewards in the form of engaged, motivated, and loyal employees.

Organizational policies also play a pivotal role in fostering trust and mutual respect. When policies are fair, transparent, and consistently applied, they send a clear message: the organization values every individual equally. Conversely, discrepancies, favoritism, or opaqueness can erode the very foundation of trust.

In essence, trust and mutual respect aren't mere aspirational goals; they're operational necessities. They influence every facet of organizational dynamics, from collaboration to innovation, and from retention to performance. Recognizing their centrality and investing in them is the first step towards a psychologically safe environment.

Open Communication

The power of open communication in fostering psychological safety cannot be overstated. It forms the bedrock upon which ideas are exchanged, concerns are voiced, and collaboration flourishes. In organizations that prioritize open communication, employees don't just talk; they feel heard.

However, open communication isn't just about speaking; it's equally about listening. Active listening, where the listener is genuinely engaged and receptive, creates an environment where employees feel valued. They become more inclined to share insights, voice concerns, and participate actively in discussions.

Training plays a crucial role in enhancing open communication. Equip employees with the skills to articulate their thoughts, manage conflicts, and provide constructive feedback. Such skills not only promote effective communication but also minimize misunderstandings and conflicts, both of which can erode psychological safety.

Furthermore, leaders have a unique role in championing open communication. When leaders are approachable, transparent, and receptive to feedback, they set a precedent for the rest of the organization. Their behavior signals that communication, in all its forms, is not just welcomed but actively encouraged.

Lastly, technological tools can bolster open communication. Whether it's collaboration platforms, feedback tools, or virtual meeting spaces, technology can bridge geographical and hierarchical divides. By leveraging these tools effectively, organizations can ensure that communication remains fluid, transparent, and inclusive, irrespective of the external environment.

Embracing Vulnerability

Vulnerability, often misconstrued as a weakness, is in reality a strength. Embracing vulnerability in the workplace is about acknowledging that nobody has all the answers. It's about recognizing and owning up to mistakes, asking for help when needed, and being open about challenges. Such behaviors, far from undermining authority or expertise, humanize individuals, making them relatable and approachable.

Leaders, given their positions of authority, can play a pivotal role in normalizing vulnerability. When leaders admit their mistakes, ask for feedback, or share their challenges, they create an environment where vulnerability is not just accepted but valued. Their behavior sends a clear message: It's okay not to be perfect.

Moreover, vulnerability fosters innovation. When employees are unburdened by the fear of judgment or retribution, they're more inclined to take risks. They're more likely to voice unconventional ideas, challenge the status quo, and push the boundaries. Such behaviors are the lifeblood of innovation and growth.

Additionally, vulnerability enhances interpersonal relationships. When individuals share their challenges, fears, or aspirations, it creates bonds of empathy. These bonds, built on mutual understanding, are the foundation of strong, cohesive teams that can weather challenges, both internal and external.

In conclusion, vulnerability isn't a liability; it's an asset. By understanding its value and weaving it into the organizational fabric, companies can foster environments where employees feel genuinely safe, valued, and inspired.

The Value of Inclusion and Diversity

Inclusion and diversity, often used interchangeably, are distinct yet interrelated pillars of psychological safety. Diversity is about representation, ensuring that the organization reflects the rich tapestry of backgrounds, experiences, and perspectives. Inclusion, on the other hand, is about ensuring that this diverse workforce feels valued, heard, and involved.

Diverse teams bring a plethora of benefits. They bring unique perspectives, leading to innovative solutions. They're better at understanding and catering to diverse customer bases. Moreover, they're often more resilient, with a broader range of experiences and skills to navigate challenges. Yet, the mere presence of diversity isn't enough. Without inclusion, diversity can become a mere tick-box exercise.

Inclusive environments recognize and value the uniqueness of every individual. They ensure that opportunities, whether for growth, learning, or leadership, are equitably distributed. They actively combat unconscious biases, ensuring that decisions, whether related to hiring, promotions, or projects, are based on merit and not prejudice.

Training, both in terms of awareness and skills, is crucial for fostering inclusion. By making employees aware of unconscious biases, and giving them tools to counteract them, organizations can ensure that inclusion isn't just a policy but a lived reality.

Lastly, metrics matter. By regularly assessing the state of inclusion and diversity, through surveys, feedback, and data analysis, organizations can ensure that they're on the right path. Such assessments, coupled with actionable insights, can drive continuous improvement, ensuring that the organization remains truly inclusive.

Chapter 5: The Antithesis: The Costs of a Toxic Environment

Stress and Burnout

In the shadow of a toxic workplace, the specters of stress and burnout loom large. Employees, constantly navigating a minefield of hostility, criticism, and fear, find their mental and emotional resources stretched to breaking point. Stress isn't merely an unpleasant byproduct of such an environment—it becomes the pervasive atmosphere, stifling potential and joy alike.

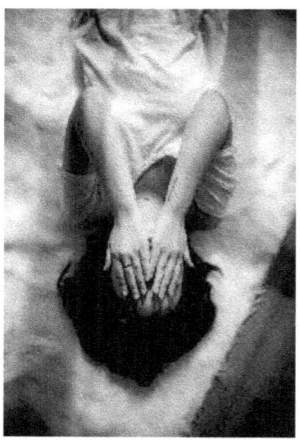

As stress accumulates, productivity dips. Tasks that were once straightforward become burdensome. Creativity and enthusiasm are overshadowed by anxiety and trepidation. Team interactions, instead of being platforms of collaboration, morph into arenas of competition and one-upmanship. The ripple effects are vast, with deteriorating work quality, missed deadlines, and escalating conflicts becoming the norm.

Burnout is the natural, albeit tragic, culmination of this escalating stress. It's characterized by extreme fatigue, cynicism, detachment, and a palpable reduction in performance. For employees who experience burnout, every workday becomes an endurance test—a relentless grind devoid of purpose or pleasure.

Furthermore, the physical repercussions of prolonged stress are significant. From sleep disturbances and weakened immune systems to more severe conditions like cardiovascular diseases, the body bears the brunt of the mind's turmoil. The cost, thus, isn't just in terms of deteriorated work performance but also in the very health and well-being of the workforce.

Organizations, too, pay a hefty price. Medical leaves, decreased productivity, and escalating healthcare costs are tangible ramifications. However, the intangible costs—the erosion of organizational reputation, the loss of talent, and the stifling of innovation—are far more detrimental in the long run.

In essence, stress and burnout are not mere occupational hazards of a toxic environment. They are harbingers of a systemic collapse—a clarion call that change is not just desirable but imperative.

The Diminishing Returns of Fear-Based Leadership

Fear-based leadership, characterized by intimidation, unpredictability, and a perpetual power play, might seem effective in the short run. Immediate compliance, rapid results, and an apparent semblance of order might give the illusion of efficacy. However, the long-term costs of such leadership far outweigh any temporary gains.

When fear is the driving force, authenticity takes a back seat. Employees, in their quest for survival, become adept at playing roles—saying what they believe the leadership wants to hear, projecting what they believe is the 'right' image, and suppressing any semblance of dissent or disagreement. This facade, while protective, is also suffocating, stifling genuine expression and innovation.

Furthermore, fear-based leadership cultivates a culture of secrecy and isolation. Information becomes a currency, hoarded by the few and denied to the many. Collaboration is replaced by caution, and trust becomes a rare commodity. Teams, instead of being cohesive units, become fractured entities, each member wary of the other.

Innovation, a crucial driver of organizational growth, is one of the first casualties of fear-based leadership. The risk-taking inherent in innovation becomes a liability in an environment where mistakes are met with retribution. The result? A stagnant organization, trapped in its ways, and resistant to change.

Morale, too, takes a nosedive. When the predominant emotions are anxiety and dread, motivation is hard to come by. Employees, instead of being ambassadors of the organization, become its silent critics—disengaged, disillusioned, and detached.

To summarize, fear-based leadership, while seemingly effective, is a ticking time bomb. Its costs, both overt and covert, are monumental, leading to a hollowed organization—devoid of trust, innovation, and genuine engagement.

The High Turnover Rate

One of the most overt indicators of a toxic work environment is a high turnover rate. When employees view their exit as a relief rather than a regret, it's a damning indictment of the prevailing organizational culture. While turnover is a natural aspect of organizational dynamics, an unusually high rate is a red flag that cannot be ignored.

High turnover disrupts the organizational rhythm. Every exit entails a loss of institutional knowledge, a disruption in team dynamics, and the logistical challenges of hiring and training replacements. The direct financial costs—recruitment, training, and lost productivity—are significant. However, the indirect costs, such as the impact on team morale, cohesion, and client relationships, can be even more detrimental.

Moreover, a high turnover rate impacts the organization's reputation in the job market. Word spreads, and soon the organization is branded as a 'toxic' workplace. Attracting top talent becomes a challenge, and even when talent is acquired, the shadow of the organization's reputation impacts their commitment and engagement.

Furthermore, every exit is a lost opportunity—a potential leader, innovator, or influencer who could have propelled the organization to greater heights. The churn also impacts the remaining employees. Watching their peers leave induces anxiety and doubt, leading to a pervasive sense of instability and insecurity.

Leadership's response to this turnover is crucial. If the exits are dismissed as routine or blamed solely on the exiting employees, it's a missed opportunity for introspection and reform. However, if they're viewed as feedback, as indicators of deeper systemic issues, they can catalyze transformative change.

In conclusion, a high turnover rate isn't just a statistic; it's a story—a narrative of discontent, disillusionment, and missed potential. How organizations interpret and respond to this story determines their trajectory—either a continual descent into toxicity or a rejuvenating ascent into positivity.

Chapter 6: Building a Psychologically Safe Environment

Leading by Example

Leadership isn't just about directing; it's about embodying the principles and values one wishes to see in the organization. A psychologically safe environment begins at the top, with leaders who demonstrate respect, empathy, and vulnerability.

Leading by example involves creating spaces where every team member feels seen and valued. It means acknowledging one's own limitations and being open to feedback. This humility makes leadership approachable, bridging the hierarchical divide and fostering mutual respect.

Furthermore, leaders set the tone for organizational interactions. When they engage in active listening, value diverse perspectives, and prioritize well-being over mere productivity, they send a clear message: people matter.

In essence, leadership's commitment to psychological safety isn't just verbal. It's a lived experience, reflected in daily interactions, decisions, and priorities. Through consistency and authenticity, leaders can lay the foundation for a nurturing, inclusive, and empowering environment.

Fostering Open Dialogue

Open dialogue is the heartbeat of a psychologically safe environment. It's the conduit through which ideas flow, concerns are addressed, and collaborative solutions emerge. An atmosphere where voices—irrespective of rank or tenure—are valued and encouraged is pivotal.

Creating platforms for such dialogues is crucial. Regular team meetings, feedback sessions, and open forums can facilitate structured conversations. However, it's equally important to encourage informal dialogues—spontaneous interactions where insights, apprehensions, and aspirations can be shared without reservation.

Moreover, fostering open dialogue also entails active listening. It's not just about speaking, but about absorbing, reflecting, and responding. By validating contributions and ensuring that feedback is constructive, organizations can ensure that dialogue isn't just frequent but also fruitful.

In conclusion, open dialogue transforms the organizational fabric. It breaks down silos, bridges divides, and fosters a sense of community. Through consistent efforts and genuine engagement, organizations can make open dialogue not an exception but the norm.

Promoting Continuous Learning

A psychologically safe environment isn't static. It evolves, adapting to changing dynamics and needs. At the core of this evolution is continuous learning— an unyielding commitment to growth, both individual and collective.

Promoting continuous learning involves multiple facets. On one hand, it's about providing opportunities—workshops, courses, and seminars where skills can be honed and horizons expanded. On the other hand, it's about fostering a mindset—a culture where learning is celebrated, curiosity is encouraged, and knowledge is shared freely.

Peer-to-peer learning sessions, mentorship programs, and learning sabbaticals can further bolster this culture. By diversifying learning avenues, organizations cater to varied learning styles and preferences, ensuring inclusivity.

Moreover, the benefits of continuous learning extend beyond skill acquisition. They permeate the very psyche of the workforce, instilling confidence, fostering adaptability, and fueling innovation.

In summary, continuous learning is the bedrock of adaptability. In a world marked by rapid changes, it's the organizations that learn, unlearn, and relearn that thrive. Through deliberate efforts and sustained commitment, organizations can ensure that learning isn't just an activity but an ethos.

Dealing with Mistakes Constructively

Mistakes are an inevitable aspect of any journey, including the organizational journey. However, it's the response to these mistakes that determines the trajectory of this journey. In a psychologically safe environment, mistakes aren't grounds for retribution but opportunities for reflection and growth.

Firstly, mistakes need to be destigmatized. An environment where errors lead to blame games, humiliation, or punitive measures is one where caution overrides innovation. Employees, in fear of repercussions, play it safe, avoiding risks and stifling creativity.

Instead, organizations should foster an analytical approach to mistakes. When an error occurs, the focus should shift from 'who' to 'why'. Root cause analyses, reflective discussions, and collaborative problem-solving can transform mistakes from setbacks to stepping stones.

Leadership plays a pivotal role in this transformation. By owning their mistakes, by ensuring that feedback is constructive rather than critical, and by prioritizing learning over blame, leaders can set the tone for the entire organization.

Furthermore, celebrating recoveries and pivots is as important as addressing mistakes. When teams rally together to rectify an error, their collaborative triumph should be acknowledged and appreciated.

In essence, mistakes, while unwelcome, are invaluable. They shed light on vulnerabilities, provide insights, and catalyze innovation. In a psychologically safe environment, they become not just tolerable but transformative.

Chapter 7: Measuring Psychological Safety

Surveys and Feedback Tools

In the intricate tapestry of organizational dynamics, understanding employee sentiment holds a place of paramount importance. Surveys and feedback tools offer a window into the collective psyche of the workforce, revealing perceptions, concerns, and areas of improvement. Properly crafted surveys weave together objective, quantifiable questions with open-ended queries, ensuring a holistic understanding of the workplace environment.

However, the true essence of feedback lies in the trust it's built upon. Assurances of confidentiality are crucial; employees need the confidence that their candid responses won't result in repercussions. This trust, once established, often translates into more honest and constructive feedback.

Feedback isn't just about collection; it's a precursor to action. When organizations actively implement changes based on feedback, it reinforces a culture of respect and responsiveness. In our digital age, real-time feedback tools, integrated into daily work, offer immediate insights, allowing organizations the agility to promptly address emerging concerns.

Here are five prominent examples of surveys and feedback tools that organizations utilize to measure and enhance psychological safety and other facets of workplace dynamics:

1. **Employee Net Promoter Score (eNPS):** This is a variation of the Net Promoter Score, a metric commonly used to gauge customer loyalty. In the employee version, staff members are asked a simple question: "On a scale of 0-10, how likely are you to recommend this company as a place to work?" Responses are then categorized into Promoters (9-10), Passives (7-8), and Detractors (0-6). The eNPS is calculated by subtracting the percentage of Detractors from the percentage of Promoters.

2. **Pulse Surveys:** Unlike annual or bi-annual surveys, pulse surveys are short, focused questionnaires sent out regularly (weekly, monthly, quarterly) to get a quick insight into employee sentiments. They are especially useful for tracking the impact of recent changes or initiatives.

3. **360-Degree Feedback:** This comprehensive feedback tool involves collecting perceptions about an individual's performance from a variety of sources, including peers, subordinates, supervisors, and sometimes even clients. The aim is to provide a holistic view of an individual's performance, strengths, and areas of improvement.

4. **Project Post-Mortems or Retrospectives:** Often used in agile work environments, these are sessions held at the end of a project or sprint to discuss what went well, what didn't, and what can be improved. It provides team members with a structured platform to provide feedback about processes, collaboration, and any challenges they faced.

5. **Suggestion Boxes and Open Forums:** While they might seem traditional, these tools still offer value in the digital age. Whether it's a physical box or a digital platform, they provide employees with an avenue to voice concerns, offer suggestions, or share innovative ideas. Modern incarnations might include anonymous digital feedback platforms or collaboration tools with dedicated channels for feedback.

Each tool, when implemented correctly and complemented by action from organizational leadership, can contribute significantly to understanding and enhancing psychological safety in the workplace.

Recognizing Subtle Indicators

Beneath the surface of any organization lies a world of unspoken cues, non-verbal communications, and subtle behaviors, all of which offer valuable insights into the prevailing psychological climate. Meetings, for instance, are more than just platforms for discussion. The dynamics therein—how often people speak, whose voices dominate, and whose remain subdued—can be mirrors reflecting the level of psychological safety.

Communication patterns outside formal settings, be they casual conversations or the nature of digital interactions, can also hint at deeper currents. Hesitations, reticence, or the propensity for closed-door discussions might suggest underlying apprehensions or fears.

Moreover, overt behaviors, such as absenteeism, turnover, or enthusiasm levels, serve as tangible indicators. Sudden shifts in these patterns often necessitate a deeper dive, uncovering the root causes that might be compromising psychological safety. For leaders, cultivating an observant and empathetic lens is essential to preempt and address these issues.

Iterative Approach to Improvement

Creating and maintaining psychological safety is a continuous endeavor, one that demands an iterative approach. Once feedback is collected, be it from formal tools or recognized subtle indicators, it should steer organizational strategies and interventions. These interventions, tailored based on feedback, could range from revisiting communication protocols to investing in team-building initiatives.

Subsequent feedback should then assess the impact of these interventions. Were they effective? Did they resonate with the employees? This cyclical method ensures that organizations remain adaptive, their strategies evolving with the ever-changing fabric of the workplace.

In an era marked by rapid transformations, organizational agility is no longer just an asset; it's a necessity. An iterative approach to psychological safety not only ensures resilience amidst change but also underscores an organization's unwavering commitment to the well-being of its employees.

Chapter 8: Case Studies

The Transformation Journey: Companies that Got it Right

Google's Aristotle Project: The Quest for the Perfect Team

In 2012, Google set out to unravel what made teams successful. This ambitious initiative was coined the Aristotle Project, a nod to the philosopher's assertion that "the whole is greater than the sum of its parts." The company meticulously examined 180 teams, collating vast amounts of data ranging from team members' educational backgrounds to their dining habits.

The results were intriguing. While most would expect the perfect blend of individual talents to be the key, it was psychological safety that took the crown. A notable instance during this study involved a manager sharing a deeply personal medical story during a team meeting. This act of vulnerability created an environment where other team members felt safe enough to share their personal challenges, ranging from emotional struggles to family issues. Over time, this environment of trust and openness translated to better collaborative results, faster problem-solving, and a more innovative approach to challenges.

What Google's leadership took from this was a renewed focus on people over processes. They realized that even with all their resources and expertise, fostering environments where individuals feel they won't be punished for mistakes, and where they can be their authentic selves, was crucial for success.

Pixar's "Braintrust" Meetings: Harnessing Collective Wisdom

Pixar, known for its blockbuster animated movies, owes a part of its resounding success to a culture that fosters candid feedback. These sessions, termed "Braintrust" meetings, emerged from the vision of co-founder Ed Catmull. Directors would present their work to a trusted group, which would then dissect the presented content with surgical precision. There's no rank in the Braintrust; whether it's a rookie or a seasoned director, feedback is always direct, cutting, yet constructive.

Consider the transformation journey of the movie "Up." The original narrative was worlds apart from what eventually graced our screens. Through multiple Braintrust sessions and the relentless pursuit of a story that resonated emotionally, "Up" underwent significant rewrites, eventually leading to its iconic narrative. It wasn't about being right but about getting it right, showcasing Pixar's commitment to excellence and the importance of psychological safety in achieving it.

The animation powerhouse attributes a significant part of its success to its culture of candid feedback. Co-founder Ed Catmull introduced "Braintrust" meetings, wherein directors present their ongoing work to a group of trusted peers. These sessions are marked by unfiltered feedback, but the environment is non-hierarchical, ensuring no authority gradient impedes genuine critique.

What makes these sessions thrive is the underlying respect and the common goal: making the movie better. For instance, the original storyline for "Up" was significantly different. It was through numerous Braintrust sessions that it morphed into the heartfelt tale we know today. By fostering a culture where feedback is a gift, Pixar consistently delivers masterpieces, making it a shining example of psychological safety driving innovation.

The Container Store: Employee First, Customer Second

The Container Store, an American retail chain offering storage solutions, might not be the first name that comes to mind when thinking about innovative corporate cultures, but it's an exemplary model of getting it right with psychological safety. Their business mantra, "Employees come first, customers second," might sound counterintuitive in the retail world, but the company's success offers a compelling argument for this philosophy.

Founder Kip Tindell introduced a unique approach to employee training and development. Unlike many retail jobs where training might last a day or two, The Container Store invests a staggering 263 hours of formal training for its first-year, full-time employees. This robust foundation ensures that each employee feels confident and competent in their role.

But it's not just about training. The company has a transparent wage policy, paying its employees nearly twice the industry average. This, combined with a comprehensive benefits package, showcases the company's commitment to its workforce. And this commitment isn't just on paper; it's felt and echoed by the employees. The Container Store has consistently ranked in Fortune's list of "100 Best Companies to Work For," a testament to its positive work environment.

Furthermore, The Container Store actively encourages open communication. Employees are not just allowed but are expected to voice their opinions, offer suggestions, and raise concerns. This open-door policy, both metaphorically and literally, has led to a wealth of grassroots innovations that have been instrumental in the company's success.

The Container Store's dedication to its employees' well-being and professional growth has had a ripple effect on customer satisfaction. Employees who feel valued, respected, and secure in their roles are naturally more inclined to go the extra mile for customers. This has resulted in a loyal customer base and impressive sales figures.

It's a reinforcing cycle: by ensuring psychological safety and well-being for its employees, The Container Store ensures that its customers are treated with the same care and respect. This philosophy underscores the profound impact that psychological safety has not just on employee satisfaction, but on the bottom line as well.

The Container Store, along with Google and Pixar, serves as a shining beacon for companies worldwide. These case studies underscore that creating environments where employees feel valued, heard, and secure leads to tangible business outcomes, from innovation and collaboration to customer satisfaction and revenue growth.

Lessons from Failures: Where Companies Went Wrong

Blackberry's Decline: Ignoring the Writing on the Wall

At its zenith, Blackberry was the darling of the mobile world. However, its decline offers a cautionary tale about the perils of ignoring external feedback and being ensconced in a bubble of perceived invincibility. As the world shifted towards touchscreens and app ecosystems, Blackberry remained obstinately committed to its keyboards and closed system.

Internal reports suggest that dissenting voices, those that recognized the changing tide, were often sidelined or silenced. The company culture became one where challenging the status quo was seen as disloyalty. This lack of psychological safety in voicing concerns and the leadership's failure to heed warnings led to Blackberry's rapid descent from market leadership.

United Airlines: Handling Crisis the Wrong Way

In 2017, United Airlines faced a PR nightmare when a video surfaced showing a passenger being forcibly dragged off an overbooked flight. The subsequent handling of the crisis compounded the company's woes. Initially, the CEO's response lacked empathy and seemed to blame the passenger.

This incident not only showcased poor external communication but hinted at deeper internal issues. Employees, fearing repercussions, opted for strict adherence to protocol over empathy and common sense. The company's culture was spotlighted, with many former and current staff sharing stories of an environment where raising concerns or deviating from the script was discouraged. The backlash United faced underscores the ripple effects of a lack of psychological safety, affecting not just internal dynamics but external perceptions and brand value.

Nokia's Complacency: Missing the Smartphone Revolution

Once a global leader in mobile phones, Nokia's tale is a classic study in missed opportunities and an inability to adapt. For much of the late 1990s and early 2000s, Nokia was the name to beat in mobile telephony. Their phones were ubiquitous, praised for their durability, user-friendly interfaces, and innovative designs. However, with the advent of the smartphone era, spearheaded by Apple's iPhone in 2007, Nokia found itself struggling to stay relevant.

Internally, Nokia's culture during its peak was characterized by complacency. There was a deep-rooted belief that their supremacy in the mobile phone market was unshakable. This overconfidence was a breeding ground for a lack of innovation. When the iPhone was launched, rather than seeing it as a game-changer, Nokia underestimated its impact, considering it a niche product that wouldn't appeal to the masses.

But there was more than just external underestimation. Employees within Nokia had seen the changing trends. Some had voiced concerns about the company's outdated operating system, Symbian, and the need for a more intuitive, touch-friendly interface. However, these voices found little traction. The culture at Nokia wasn't conducive to challenging established ideas. Their considerable market share gave a false sense of security, and those who suggested significant overhauls or pivots were often deemed alarmists.

By the time Nokia realized its missteps and tried to correct course, collaborating with Microsoft to launch Windows-powered smartphones, it was too late. The market had shifted, consumer preferences had evolved, and Nokia, once a titan of its industry, found itself playing catch-up.

This is not merely a tale of technological obsolescence but a profound lesson in the importance of psychological safety. Had Nokia fostered an environment where dissenting voices, innovative ideas, and challenges to the status quo were encouraged and heeded, its trajectory might have been vastly different.

Nokia's story, juxtaposed with those of Blackberry and United Airlines, underscores that regardless of industry or market position, the absence of psychological safety can lead to tunnel vision, missed opportunities, and eventually, decline. Such environments stifle innovation, prevent agility, and render organizations vulnerable to rapidly changing market dynamics.

Chapter 9: Challenges and Misunderstandings

Overemphasis on Positivity: Ignoring Constructive Conflict

In the quest for fostering psychological safety, a potential pitfall is the inadvertent suppression of any form of conflict, assuming that all conflict is harmful. However, this notion overlooks the concept of constructive conflict—a type of conflict where differing viewpoints and ideas clash, often leading to innovative solutions and growth. Constructive conflict can be a catalyst for creativity, pushing teams to challenge their perspectives and think outside the box. When organizations overly stress the importance of positivity, they risk curbing these beneficial forms of disagreement. A harmonious environment is indeed desirable, but not at the cost of silencing crucial dialogues that can drive progress.

Case: Zappos and the Holacracy Model

Zappos, the online shoe and clothing retailer, has always been known for its unique corporate culture. In 2013, CEO Tony Hsieh made a significant shift by adopting the Holacracy model—a management-free corporate structure where roles are defined around work rather than people, and employees have high autonomy.

Initially, this new structure was seen as a breakthrough, emphasizing positivity, open dialogue, and self-governance. However, over time, some cracks began to show. One of the unintended consequences was that without a traditional management structure, employees often found it challenging to navigate disagreements or conflicts. There was a cultural push to maintain a positive atmosphere, which inadvertently meant that constructive conflicts—those that lead to growth and innovation—were often avoided.

Employees began to express that, in the absence of clear guidelines on how to navigate disagreements within this flat structure, they sometimes felt unsure of voicing dissenting opinions or engaging in debates. While the intention was to create an environment free of the politics and power dynamics typical in hierarchical organizations, the overemphasis on maintaining a consistently positive environment led to the silencing of essential conflicts that drive innovation and improvement.

Complacency: The Risk of Overdoing Safety

Psychological safety, at its essence, encourages an environment where individuals feel secure and respected, free to express their thoughts without fear of retribution. However, there's a thin line between creating a safe environment and fostering a culture of complacency. When teams become too comfortable or assured in their current status, they might resist change or innovation. This complacency can be a silent killer for organizations, particularly in industries where technological advancement and evolution are rapid. A culture that is "too safe" might deter employees from taking necessary risks, exploring uncharted territories, or challenging long-standing assumptions, all of which are vital for sustained business growth.

Case: Kodak's Reluctance to Embrace Digital

Eastman Kodak Company, commonly known as Kodak, was once synonymous with photography. For decades, they held a dominant position in the film photography market. As the 20th century neared its end, the winds of change in the form of digital photography began to blow. However, Kodak's internal environment didn't mirror this external shift.

Inside Kodak, there was an environment that could be described as "too safe." Employees felt secure in their roles, and there was a sense of complacency about the company's dominant market position. While this safety led to employee satisfaction, it also inadvertently bred an environment resistant to change. Kodak did not entirely ignore digital photography; in fact, they had developed a digital camera prototype as early as 1975. However, there was a reluctance to shift the company's focus from film to digital, primarily driven by the success and profitability of the film business.

This culture of complacency meant that risks and radical changes were not encouraged. The prevailing sentiment was to stick with what had always worked. Employees, despite recognizing the potential of digital, felt that their primary allegiance was to film—Kodak's bread and butter.

By the time Kodak recognized the magnitude of the digital revolution, they were trailing behind competitors. Their delayed entry into the digital market and the burden of maintaining a now-obsolete film business led to significant financial struggles, culminating in a bankruptcy filing in 2012.

Kodak's story is a cautionary tale of the dangers of overemphasizing safety to the point of complacency. While psychological safety is vital, it's equally essential to ensure it doesn't lead to inertia, preventing companies from adapting to changing market dynamics.

In conclusion, while the journey to foster psychological safety is imperative for modern companies, it's equally crucial to recognize potential pitfalls. Emphasizing positivity shouldn't come at the cost of stifling constructive conflict, and creating a safe environment shouldn't translate to complacency. Balancing these aspects is the key to truly harnessing the power of psychological safety in the workplace.

Chapter 10: The Future of Psychological Safety

The Digital Age: Remote Work and Virtual Teams

As the world transitions deeper into the digital age, the very fabric of workplace interactions is changing. The rise of remote work and the proliferation of virtual teams are redefining traditional concepts of the workspace. While these changes offer flexibility and a broader talent pool, they also bring forth new challenges in maintaining psychological safety.

Case Study: GitLab and Asynchronous Communication

GitLab, a complete DevOps platform, stands out as a company that has wholly embraced remote work since its inception. With employees scattered globally, GitLab has been a forerunner in building a culture of trust and psychological safety in a remote environment.

One of GitLab's core strategies is the emphasis on asynchronous communication. This means that instead of immediate responses, team members have the flexibility to respond in their own time. This approach respects diverse time zones, personal schedules, and work rhythms. Asynchronous communication ensures that employees don't feel the pressure to be "always on," thereby reducing burnout and stress.

GitLab's transparent culture, evident in its publicly available handbook, further promotes psychological safety. Every employee, regardless of their geographic location, has a clear understanding of the company's values, processes, and expectations, which removes ambiguity and fosters trust.

Societal Shifts: The Changing Landscape of Work

The 21st century has witnessed unparalleled societal shifts, with a growing emphasis on individual rights, inclusivity, and work-life balance. These societal changes, coupled with global events like the COVID-19 pandemic, are reshaping what employees expect from their workplaces.

Case Study: Patagonia and Work-Life Integration

Outdoor clothing company Patagonia has been at the forefront of recognizing and adapting to these shifts. They've championed the idea of work-life integration, rather than just work-life balance. Their on-site child care center, generous parental leave policies, and encouragement for employees to catch a surf or go hiking during work hours exemplify this philosophy.

Patagonia's approach acknowledges that employees are not just workers but whole individuals with families, hobbies, and passions. By creating an environment where employees can seamlessly blend their professional and personal lives, Patagonia ensures that their staff doesn't feel torn between work and personal commitments, thereby enhancing psychological safety.

Continuous Learning: The Ever-Evolving Nature of Safety

In an ever-changing world, the definition of psychological safety itself will evolve. Companies need to commit to continuous learning, ensuring that their understanding of safety remains current and relevant to the shifting dynamics of the workplace.

Case Study: Microsoft's Cultural Shift Under Satya Nadella

When Satya Nadella took the helm at Microsoft in 2014, he was faced with an organization that was once an industry leader but had become somewhat stagnant. Recognizing the need for a cultural overhaul, Nadella introduced the concept of a "growth mindset" – a philosophy rooted in the belief that talents can be developed through hard work, good strategies, and input from others.

This shift wasn't just a top-down directive. Microsoft introduced a range of programs and initiatives to nurture this mindset among its employees, emphasizing learning from failures and celebrating experimentation. Feedback mechanisms were strengthened, and leaders were trained to be more receptive to inputs, even if they were critical.

Under Nadella's leadership, Microsoft transformed from a company that knew it all to a company that wants to learn it all. This transition has been instrumental in reestablishing Microsoft's position at the forefront of technology innovation, illustrating the power of continuous learning in fostering psychological safety and organizational success.

In conclusion, as the fabric of our societies and workplaces changes, so too will the nuances of psychological safety. Forward-thinking companies will be those that not only recognize these shifts but actively integrate them into their organizational ethos, ensuring that they remain relevant, competitive, and above all, places where individuals feel valued and safe.

Chapter 11: Implementing Psychological Safety in Organizations

The Importance of Leadership in Cultivating Safety

Leadership, often viewed as the backbone of any organization, plays an indispensable role in shaping its culture. Leaders, by virtue of their positions, can either be enablers or barriers to psychological safety. Their actions, words, and decisions set the tone for the rest of the organization. When leaders actively promote open dialogue, admit their mistakes, and show vulnerability, they send a clear message: It's okay to be human here.

Secondly, the leader's role isn't just about personal behavior; it's about setting the structural framework for the entire organization. This includes policies, communication channels, and performance metrics. By weaving psychological safety into these structural elements, leaders can ensure that the organization's machinery actively supports and rewards safe behaviors.

However, leadership's influence on psychological safety isn't just a top-down phenomenon. By promoting leaders from within teams that have already internalized the principles of psychological safety, organizations can organically foster this environment. Such leaders, having experienced the benefits of psychological safety firsthand, become its most vocal and effective advocates.

Moreover, continuous leadership training is essential. Just as industries evolve, so does our understanding of psychological safety and its best practices. Regular training ensures that leaders are equipped with the latest tools and insights to foster a culture of safety and trust.

Lastly, leadership in the context of psychological safety is also about accountability. Leaders need to hold themselves and others accountable for maintaining a safe environment. This accountability, combined with the other elements, ensures that psychological safety isn't just a buzzword, but a lived reality for every employee.

Strategies to Promote Open Communication

Open communication forms the bedrock of psychological safety. In its absence, misunderstandings thrive, mistrust festers, and creativity is stifled. But promoting open communication isn't just about removing barriers; it's about actively fostering channels that encourage free expression. For starters, organizations can create platforms where employees can voice their concerns anonymously. Such platforms offer a safe space for those apprehensive about direct confrontation.

Beyond anonymity, regular town-hall meetings, where leadership addresses concerns, shares updates, and most importantly, listens, can go a long way. Here, leaders have the chance to actively demonstrate their commitment to psychological safety by addressing concerns and acting on feedback.

Training is another avenue to bolster open communication. By offering employees tools and techniques to communicate effectively, especially in challenging situations, organizations can reduce misunderstandings and conflicts. This training should encompass not just verbal communication but also non-verbal cues, which often convey more than words.

Encouraging cross-departmental interactions can further enhance open communication. When employees from diverse teams interact, they bring unique perspectives to the table. These interactions, whether formal or informal, can lead to innovative solutions and a broader understanding of the organization.

Lastly, feedback mechanisms shouldn't just be top-down. Peer reviews and feedback, when done constructively, can offer insights that hierarchical structures might miss. By embedding a culture of constructive feedback, organizations ensure that communication flows freely in all directions.

Building Trust Through Transparency and Accountability

Trust, like a delicate plant, needs the right environment to flourish. In organizations, this environment is often shaped by transparency and accountability. When leadership is transparent about decisions, strategies, and even failures, they lay the foundation for trust. Employees, when in the know, feel valued and involved, leading to a stronger sense of belonging.

However, transparency shouldn't be selective. It needs to encompass both the good and the bad. When organizations are transparent about challenges or mistakes, they demonstrate humility and openness. Such behaviors signal to employees that it's okay to be fallible, leading to a culture where mistakes are viewed as learning opportunities.

Accountability, the close sibling of transparency, further fortifies trust. When employees see that actions have consequences and that everyone, irrespective of their position, is held to the same standards, they feel a sense of fairness. This equitable environment is crucial for psychological safety.

Regular check-ins, both formal and informal, can enhance accountability. When employees know that their progress will be reviewed and that they'll have opportunities to discuss challenges, they're more likely to remain committed and engaged.

In conclusion, trust is the glue that binds teams and organizations. By championing transparency and accountability, organizations can ensure that this bond remains strong, paving the way for a culture rooted in psychological safety.

The Role of HR in Upholding Psychological Safety

Human Resources (HR) isn't just about hiring, policies, and paperwork. In the context of psychological safety, HR plays a pivotal role as both the guardian and promoter. Firstly, HR is often the first touchpoint for employees. By ensuring that the onboarding process introduces new hires to the importance of psychological safety, HR can set the right tone from the outset.

Training, as mentioned earlier, is crucial for psychological safety. HR, with its insights into organizational dynamics and employee needs, is best positioned to curate or source training that addresses specific challenges. Whether it's communication, conflict resolution, or leadership training, HR can be the driving force behind these initiatives.

Moreover, HR can be the bridge between employees and leadership. By creating platforms for feedback, addressing grievances, and being approachable, HR can ensure that the lines of communication remain open. Such openness is crucial, especially in situations where employees might feel hesitant to approach their immediate superiors.

Furthermore, HR policies can either foster or hinder psychological safety. By regularly revising policies to ensure they align with the principles of psychological safety, HR can ensure that the organization's structural framework supports its cultural aspirations.

Lastly, HR, with its unique position, can be the watchdog for psychological safety. By regularly surveying employees, analyzing trends, and acting on insights, HR can ensure that the organization remains committed to its goal of fostering a safe, inclusive, and nurturing environment.

Continuous Assessment and Iteration

Psychological safety, like any organizational endeavor, requires continuous assessment and iteration. What works in one context or time might not be as effective in another. Regular surveys, ideally anonymized, can offer insights into the current state of psychological safety within the organization. These insights, when acted upon, demonstrate the organization's commitment to its employees' well-being.

Beyond surveys, focus group discussions can offer deeper insights. By bringing together employees from diverse teams and hierarchies, organizations can tap into a rich reservoir of experiences and suggestions. Such discussions, facilitated by neutral parties, can lead to actionable strategies that can further bolster psychological safety.

However, assessment isn't just about gathering data; it's about acting on it. Organizations need to be agile, ready to iterate on strategies based on feedback. This agility not only enhances psychological safety but also signals to employees that their voices matter.

Additionally, looking outside can offer valuable insights. By staying updated on the latest research, best practices, and trends related to psychological safety, organizations can ensure that their strategies are not just effective but also relevant.

In conclusion, the journey towards psychological safety isn't a destination but a continuous process. With regular assessment, feedback, and iteration, organizations can ensure that they remain on the right path, adapting and evolving as needed.

As we conclude this chapter, it's evident that implementing psychological safety is a multifaceted endeavor. From leadership to HR, from transparency to continuous assessment, each element plays a critical role. The subsequent chapters will delve deeper into real-world case studies, offering insights into how organizations, big and small, have navigated this journey.

Chapter 4: The Ripple Effects

Improved Team Collaboration

The power of a cohesive team cannot be underestimated. When psychological safety is entrenched within a team, the walls of hesitation crumble, replaced by bridges of collaboration. Members begin to feel a sense of security, knowing that their contributions will be respected and that any potential errors won't be met with undue criticism.

This environment of mutual trust and respect facilitates seamless communication. Team members actively seek feedback, not as a measure of judgment but as a tool for improvement. The fear of overshadowing or being overshadowed recedes, and what emerges is a harmonious orchestration where each member plays their part to perfection.

Moreover, when each individual feels safe and acknowledged, they tend to invest more in the team's success. Their commitment to the team's goals becomes unwavering, resulting in a collective effort that far surpasses the sum of its parts. Regular team rituals, feedback sessions, and collaborative tools further amplify this sense of unity and purpose.

The significance of such collaboration is profound. Projects are executed efficiently, roadblocks are navigated with collective wisdom, and team successes are celebrated as shared triumphs. In essence, a psychologically safe environment doesn't just improve team collaboration; it elevates it to an art form.

Enhancing Creativity and Innovation

Creativity thrives where there's freedom—freedom to think, to question, and to explore. In a psychologically safe environment, this freedom becomes a staple. Employees feel empowered to step outside the proverbial box, to challenge existing norms, and to introduce novel ideas.

The absence of fear of ridicule or rejection means that even unconventional or seemingly outlandish ideas get a platform. Often, these are the ideas that lead to groundbreaking innovations. The diverse perspectives inherent in an inclusive environment further enrich this pool of creativity. When diverse minds brainstorm, the resulting mosaic of ideas can be both breathtaking and revolutionary.

Leaders play a crucial role in this matrix. By fostering a culture that celebrates creativity, by being open to new ideas, and by creating platforms where such ideas can be showcased and refined, they can catalyze innovation. Regular innovation workshops, hackathons, or even informal brainstorming sessions can be instrumental in this regard.

Moreover, recognizing and rewarding creativity sends a powerful message. It reiterates the organization's commitment to innovation and encourages more employees to participate in this creative journey. Over time, what emerges is not just a series of innovations but an innovation-driven ethos that defines the organization's very identity.

Strengthening Employee Retention

The link between psychological safety and employee retention is direct and powerful. In a world where talent wars are intense, retaining top talent becomes as crucial as acquiring it. A psychologically safe environment acts as a magnetic force, binding employees to the organization.

Such an environment addresses the core human need for respect, belonging, and purpose. When employees feel valued, not just for their contributions but for who they are, their allegiance to the organization solidifies. The mutual trust ensures that even during challenging times, employees are more likely to stick around, believing in the organization's vision and its commitment to them.

Moreover, psychologically safe environments promote growth—both personal and professional. When employees see opportunities to learn, to innovate, and to climb the organizational ladder, their motivation to stay amplifies. Regular feedback sessions, growth-centric training, and transparent promotion policies further bolster this retention drive.

It's also worth noting that employee retention has cascading benefits. Retained employees possess deep organizational knowledge, which aids in smoother operations and informed decision-making. Their consistent presence adds to team stability and cohesion. In essence, by investing in psychological safety, organizations don't just retain employees; they retain organizational wisdom and cohesion.

Fostering Resilience and Adaptability

The corporate landscape is punctuated by change—technological shifts, market dynamics, or global events. Resilience and adaptability aren't just virtues; they're survival skills. A psychologically safe environment serves as a crucible where these skills are forged.

In such an environment, challenges are not shunned but embraced as learning opportunities. The collective mindset shifts from fear of failure to a quest for learning. When mistakes are made, they're dissected for insights rather than used as fodder for blame. This perspective, where challenges become stepping stones, is the cornerstone of resilience.

Adaptability, too, flourishes in psychologically safe environments. Employees, unburdened by the fear of judgment, are more willing to learn, unlearn, and relearn. They're more receptive to feedback, more eager to upskill, and more agile in pivoting as per organizational needs.

Furthermore, the collaborative spirit inherent in such environments ensures that adaptability becomes a collective endeavor. Teams rally together to navigate changes, sharing insights, resources, and strategies. Regular training sessions, workshops, and change management protocols further enable this adaptive journey.

In essence, resilience and adaptability aren't just outcomes of psychological safety; they're its living testimonials. They showcase the transformative power of an environment where safety, respect, and growth coalesce.

Page 135

Chapter 12: Conclusion

The Ongoing Journey

Anecdote: The Metamorphosis of Marathon Runners

Consider for a moment the transformational journey of a marathon runner. It's a rainy morning in Boston, and Sarah, a first-time marathoner, stands at the starting line of the historic Boston Marathon. With a blend of excitement and trepidation, she takes her first step, feeling the weight of the road ahead and the countless hours of training behind her.

Page 136

By mile 5, the rain clears, and she is buoyed by the cheering crowds. A sense of accomplishment swells in her chest, but she's acutely aware that there's so much more to traverse. At mile 20, known infamously as "Heartbreak Hill," Sarah feels the ache in her limbs, the breaths coming harder, yet she digs deep into her reserves, driven by her vision of the finish line.

The world of organizational psychology is no different. Introducing and maintaining psychological safety is like Sarah's maiden marathon journey. Initial milestones might be reached, bringing with them the euphoria of accomplishment. However, just like Heartbreak Hill, organizations will face challenges that test their commitment. But if they persevere, keep adapting, and stay resilient, the rewards - an inclusive, innovative, and productive workspace - await at the end.

Committing to a Better Workplace

Anecdote: From Broken Windows to Blossoming Streets

In the late 20th century, New York City was grappling with rising crime rates. The "Broken Window" theory postulated that visible signs of disorder, like a simple broken window, could lead to an escalation of criminal activity. If small acts of neglect or damage were left unaddressed, they sent a signal that no one cared, prompting a decline in community morale and an uptick in serious crimes.

In the early '90s, the city put this theory into practice. Instead of solely focusing on major crimes, authorities began clamping down on smaller infractions, from graffiti to minor subway offenses. The streets started to change; dilapidated buildings were refurbished, parks rejuvenated, and subway cars cleaned. As these "broken windows" were fixed, a remarkable transformation occurred. Not only did minor offenses drop, but so did major crimes.

Now, let's pivot this idea to an organizational setting. Imagine a company where small issues - a snide comment left unaddressed, a team member regularly sidelined in meetings, or an overworked employee's concerns brushed under the rug - are the "broken windows." These seemingly minor transgressions can fester and lead to more significant problems: declining morale, lack of trust, and stifled innovation. However, by committing to address these issues, much like New York City, organizations can transform. By fixing their "broken windows," they pave the way for a culture of respect, trust, and collaboration.

In conclusion, while the road to a psychologically safe workplace is filled with challenges and requires ongoing effort, the outcome is worth the journey. Like Sarah, who crosses her finish line with a sense of unparalleled achievement, organizations can look back on their journey with pride, knowing they have crafted a space where every individual feels valued, heard, and safe.

Chapter 13: Additional Resources and Readings

Additional readings

1. The New York Times Magazine

   Title: "What Google Learned From Its Quest to Build the Perfect Team"

   Author: Charles Duhigg

   Summary: The article dives deep into Google's multi-year study to figure out why some teams thrive while others falter. A significant outcome was the identification of psychological safety as the most critical factor in building a successful team.

2. Harvard Business Review (HBR)

Title: "High-Performing Teams Need Psychological Safety. Here's How to Create It"

Author: Laura Delizonna

Summary: This HBR article focuses on the importance of psychological safety in high-performing teams. Delizonna gives practical advice on fostering an environment where team members feel secure enough to take risks, voice their opinions, and ask judgment-free questions.

3. Forbes

   Title: "The One Requirement For A Psychologically Safe Workplace"

   Author: Tracy Brower

   Summary: The piece emphasizes the role of trust in creating psychologically safe workplaces. Brower provides insights into building trust among teams and its ripple effect in enhancing productivity and innovation.

4. The Guardian

   Title: "Why we need psychologically safe workspaces – and how to create them"

   Summary: This article explores the consequences of not having psychologically safe workspaces, from mental health issues to decreased productivity. It also offers tips for employers and team leaders on how to foster such an environment.

5. Inc. Magazine

Title: "How to Build Psychological Safety for Your Team, According to Harvard"

Author: Scott Mautz

Summary: Drawing from research and practical examples, this article dives into ways leaders can build and maintain psychological safety within their teams, ensuring an environment conducive to innovation and collaboration.

Research Papers

1. Edmondson, A. (1999). Psychological Safety and Learning Behavior in Work Teams. *Administrative Science Quarterly, 44*(2), 350-383.

2. Kahn, W. A. (1990). Psychological Conditions of Personal Engagement and Disengagement at Work. *Academy of Management Journal, 33*(4), 692-724.

3. Newman, A., Donohue, R., & Eva, N. (2017). Psychological safety: A systematic review of the literature. *Human Resource Management Review, 27*(3), 521-535.

4. Duhigg, C. (2016). What Google Learned From Its Quest to Build the Perfect Team. *The New York Times Magazine*.

5. Delizonna, L. (2017). High-Performing Teams Need Psychological Safety. Here's How to Create It. *Harvard Business Review*.

6. Woolley, A. W., Chabris, C. F., Pentland, A., Hashmi, N., & Malone, T. W. (2010). Evidence for a Collective Intelligence Factor in the Performance of Human Groups. *Science, 330*(6004), 686-688.

7. Frazier, M. L., Fainshmidt, S., Klinger, R. L., Pezeshkan, A., & Vracheva, V. (2017). Psychological Safety: A Meta-Analytic Review and Extension. *Personnel Psychology, 70*(1), 113-165.

8. Carmeli, A., Brueller, D., & Dutton, J. E. (2009). Learning behaviours in the workplace: The role of high-quality interpersonal relationships and psychological safety. *Systems Research and Behavioral Science, 26*(1), 81-98.

9. Nembhard, I. M., & Edmondson, A. C. (2006). Making it safe: The effects of leader inclusiveness and professional status on psychological safety and improvement efforts in health care teams. *Journal of Organizational Behavior, 27*(7), 941-966.

10. Detert, J. R., & Burris, E. R. (2007). Leadership behavior and employee voice: Is the door really open?. *Academy of Management Journal, 50*(4), 869-884.

11. Tucker, A. L., Nembhard, I. M., & Edmondson, A. C. (2007). Implementing new practices: An empirical study of organizational learning in hospital intensive care units. *Management Science, 53*(6), 894-907.

12. Cullen-Lester, K. L., Leroy, H., Gerbasi, A., & Nishii, L. (2016). An exploration of the benefits of network diversity for team innovativeness. *Journal of Applied Psychology, 101*(4), 527.

13. Hirak, R., Peng, A. C., Carmeli, A., & Schaubroeck, J. M. (2012). Linking leader inclusiveness to work unit performance: The importance of psychological safety and learning from failures. *Leadership Quarterly, 23*(1), 107-117.

14. Singer, S. J., & Edmondson, A. C. (2008). When learning and performance are at odds: Confronting the tension. *Harvard Business School Organizational Behavior Unit Working Paper*, (09-035).

15. Baer, M., & Frese, M. (2003). Innovation is not enough: Climates for initiative and psychological safety, process innovations, and firm performance. *Journal of Organizational Behavior, 24*(1), 45-68.

About the Author

About the Author

David C. Winegar is a seasoned professional with over a quarter-century of experience in human development within multinational environments. He holds an MBA from the University of Pittsburgh, specializing in organizational behavior and e-business. As the visionary founder of two technology ventures, he successfully secured multimillion-dollar investments, pioneering innovations in both the travel and mobile sectors.

For the past 2 decades, Mr. Winegar has led his training and development firm, with a core focus on leadership enhancement and sales strategies. This endeavor has seen him facilitate learning experiences for thousands across more than seventy nations. His proficiencies encompass business coaching, strategic presentation crafting, conversational intelligence, and pitch development. Through his multifaceted career, David has established himself as a global thought leader in the corporate training sphere.